Y0-DLA-220

YOUR SKIN and HAIR

Joan Iveson-Iveson

Illustrated by Bill Donohoe

The Bookwright Press
New York · 1986

All About You

Your Eyes
Your Hands and Feet
Your Health
Your Nose and Ears
Your Skin and Hair
Your Teeth

Acknowledgments

Sally and Richard Greenhill, p.4, 8, 10, 13, 17, 18, 19, 21; J. Merrett p.22, 23; Wayland Picture Library p.15, 20.

First published in the United States in 1986 by
The Bookwright Press
387 Park Avenue South
New York, NY 10016

First published in 1985 by Wayland (Publishers) Limited
61 Western Road, Hove, East Sussex BN3 1JD, England
© 1985 Wayland (Publishers) Limited

ISBN 0–531–18043–3
Library of Congress Catalog Card Number: 85–72746

Phototypeset by Kalligraphics Limited, Redhill, Surrey
Printed in Italy by G. Canale and C.S.p.A., Turin

Contents

Your skin and hair   4
What is your skin made of?   6
How does your skin work?   8
Keeping warm, staying cool   10
Taking care of your skin   12
The hair on your head   14
The hair on your body   16
How quickly does hair grow?   18
What kind of hair do you have?   20
Taking care of your hair   22
Glossary   24
Index   25

Your skin and hair

Your skin is one of the most important parts of your body. It covers you from head to toe and it does many things that help to keep you healthy and happy.

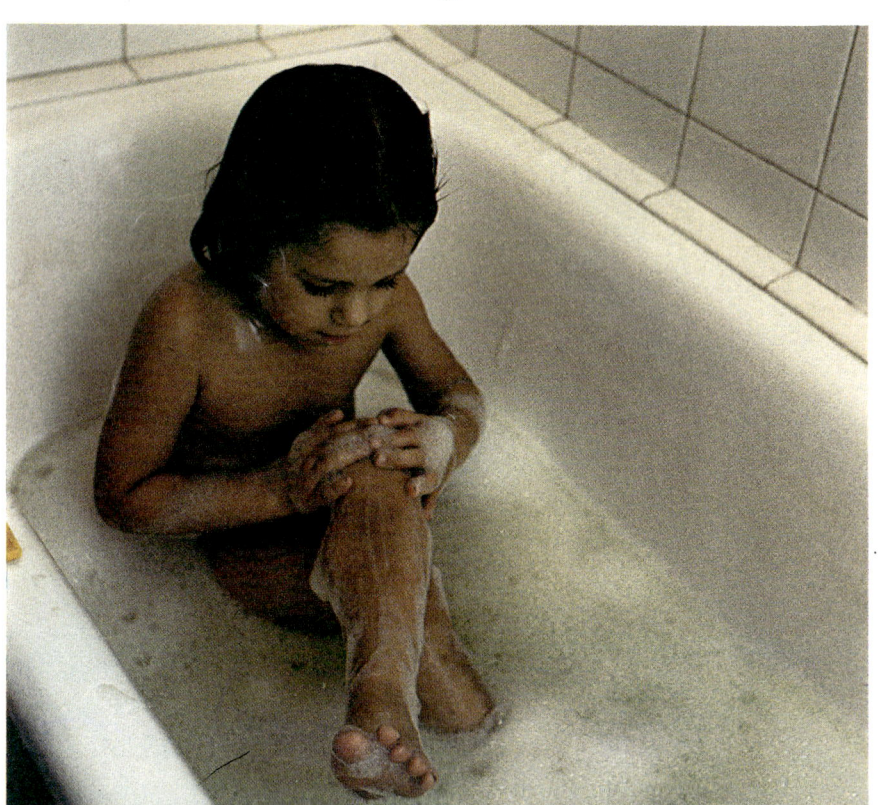

It is **sensitive** to changes in the temperature and it is sensitive to touch. It is waterproof, so water runs off it when you're in the bath. It keeps the heat in when you're cold and lets it out when you're hot. It holds in all the inside parts of your body and it keeps out all the germs.

Your hair grows out of your skin. It grows nearly everywhere on your body, except on the palms of your hands, on the soles of your feet, on your eyelids and on your lips. On your head you can have as many as 150,000 hairs. They can be curly, straight, blond, brown, red or black.

What is your skin made of?

Let's take a closer look at your skin. It is made of several layers, but on your eyelids and lips it is only ½ millimeter (.02 in) thick. The outer layer of the skin, which you can see, is called the epidermis. The layer beneath is the dermis and this is packed with **veins**, **nerve endings** and **hair follicles**. Below this there is a layer of fat.

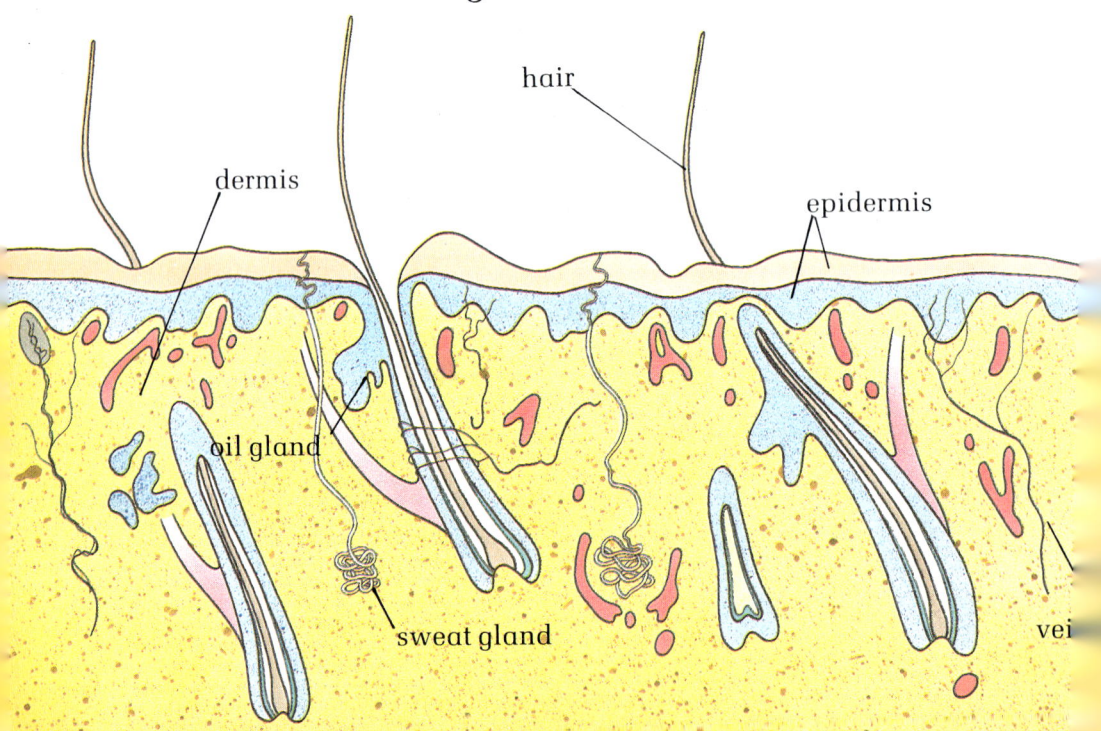

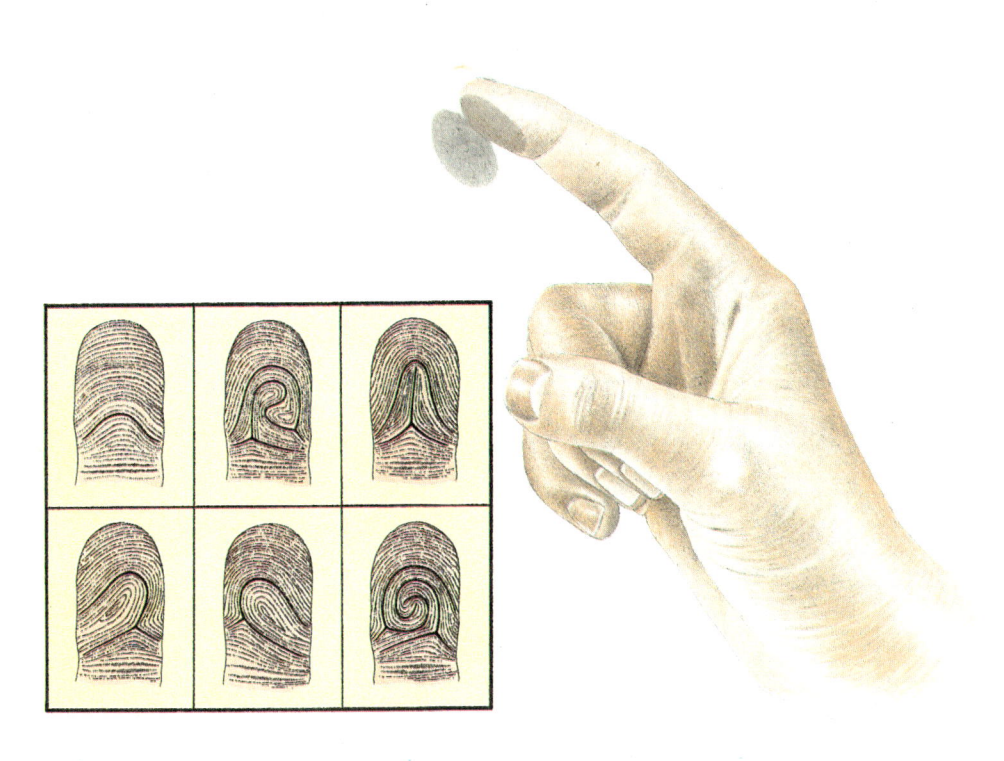

The color of your skin depends on how much **melanin** there is in it. Dark-brown skin has more melanin in it than pale skin.

At the end of your fingers your skin forms patterns of lines. If you rub the ends of your fingers with a pencil and then press each one onto a piece of paper you will be able to see your fingerprints. There are different kinds of prints, as you can see in the picture, and no two people have the same ones.

How does your skin work?

When you cut or scratch your skin, your body immediately tries to mend it. More blood rushes to that area and a **clot** forms to cover the hole in the skin. A scratch or graze like the one in the picture would usually **heal** without leaving a mark. But a cut that went as deep as the dermis would leave a mark on your skin called a scar.

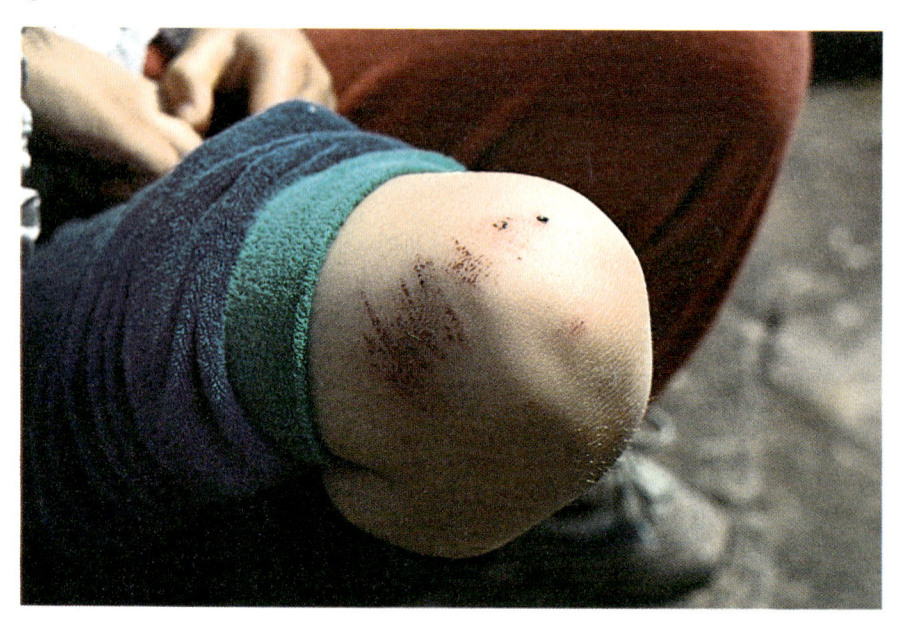

Your skin is also **elastic**. When you yawn, or bend your elbows or knees, your skin stretches and then goes back to its original shape.

Your skin is waterproof. Water runs off your body when you wash yourself; it does not soak in. This is because your skin has natural oils in it, which come from **glands** in the layers of your skin. The oils mix with sweat to form a waterproof cover.

Keeping warm, staying cool

Your skin helps to keep your body at an even temperature. When you get very hot you sweat from small glands under your skin. These little drops of salty water on your skin **evaporate** and this helps you to cool down. You need to drink a lot to replace the liquid you are losing.

When you are cold, the fine hairs on the surface of your skin stand on end. It is just the way a bird fluffs out its feathers to keep itself warm.

Your skin is also very sensitive to touch. Just below the surface there are hundreds of nerve endings, which collect information and send it to your brain. You can feel the lightest touch of a feather or the sharpest prick of a pin. This boy has pricked his finger on a thorn while picking blackberries.

Taking care of your skin

Take care of the outer layer of your skin by washing every day. This removes dead **cells**, sweat and oils from the surface of your skin. Make sure that you dry your skin well, particularly where two skin surfaces meet and rub against each other, for example between your toes.

Always remember to wash cuts and grazes before sticking on an adhesive bandage.

Your skin relies on a good diet to keep it healthy. So make sure you eat plenty of fresh fruit and vegetables. Try to eat fewer sweet things and fatty foods.

Take care always to protect your skin from anything that may harm it. Never pick up anything hot; don't sit in the sun for very long; wear warm clothes in winter.

Getting enough sleep and exercise is important too. Exercise helps increase the blood supply to the tissues of the skin.

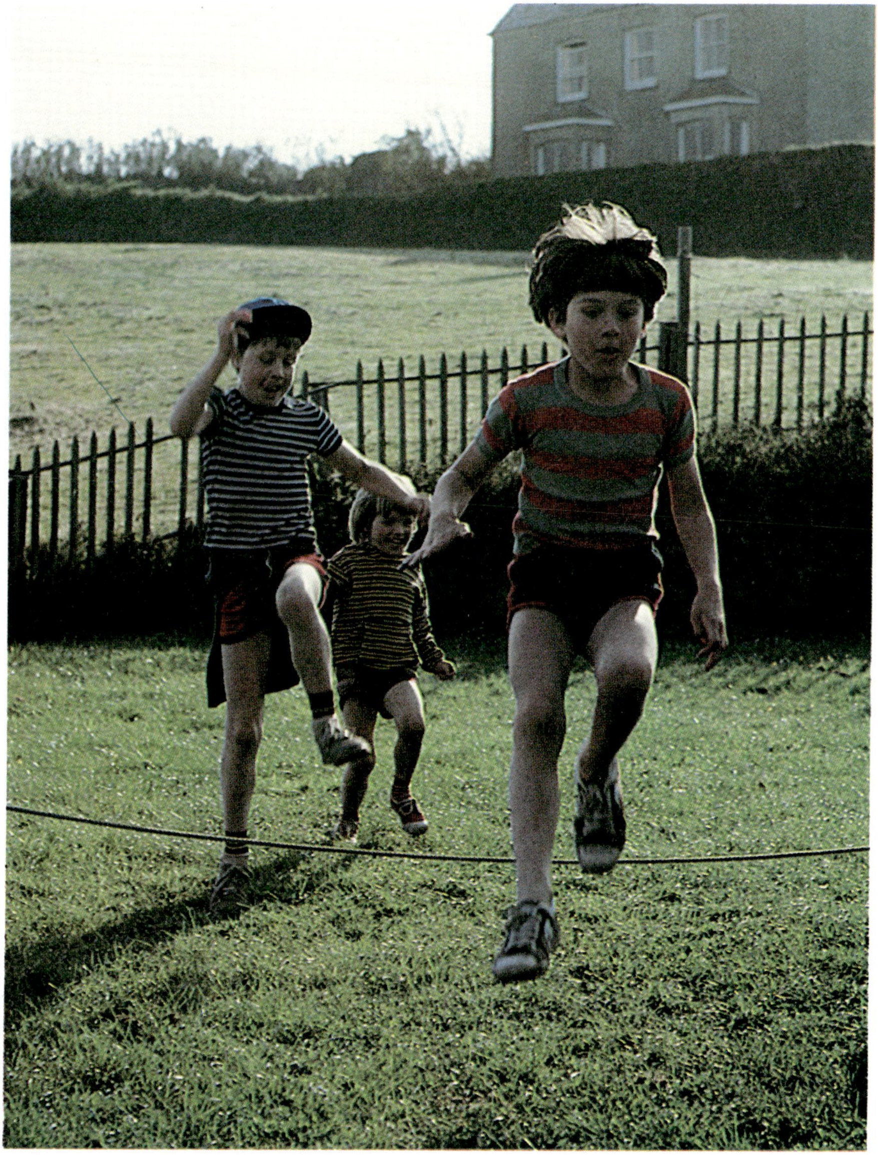

The hair on your head

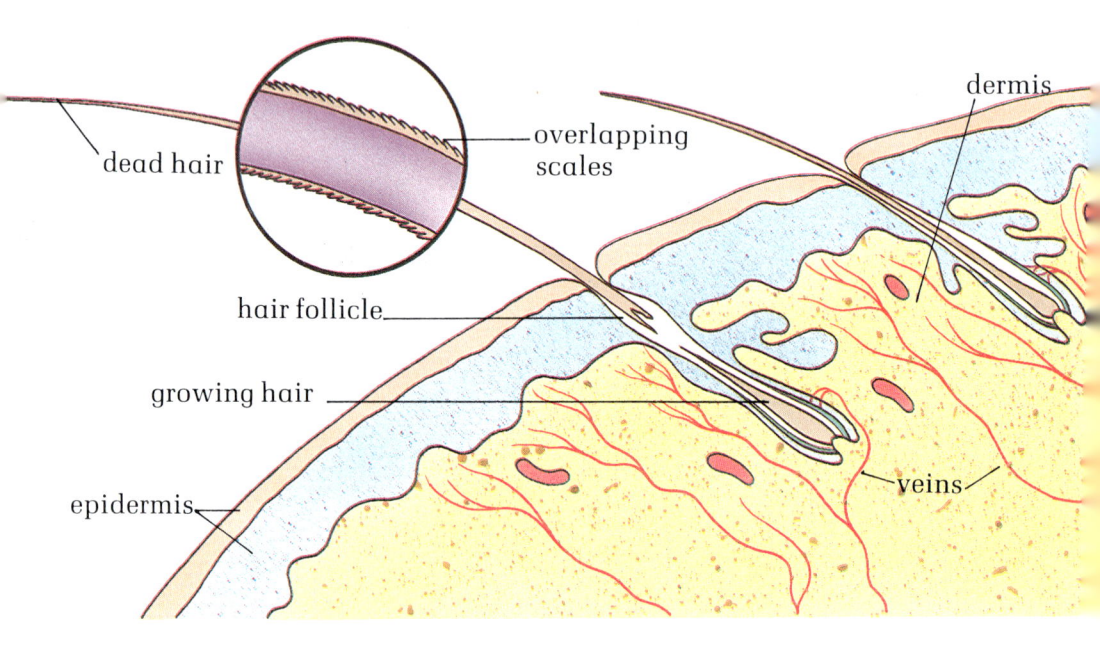

dermis
overlapping scales
dead hair
hair follicle
growing hair
epidermis
veins

Your hair is made from special cells in your skin. It begins to grow even before you are born. As you can see from this picture, it grows from beneath the surface of your **scalp**. The outside of each hair is made of clear, overlapping scales. Each hair has a root and a little **muscle**, which can make your hair "stand on end" when you are frightened.

At the bottom of every hair there is an oil gland. This pushes oil onto the surface of your skin. The oil keeps each hair smooth and shiny. If the glands make too much oil your hair gets greasy.

Every day you lose lots of hairs from your head, but they all grow back again. Some people go bald as they get older, like this man. This is because the speed at which the hair grows back gets slower, so that the hairs fall out faster than they grow back.

The hair on your body

Millions and millions of years ago human beings had thick hair all over their bodies. If you look at your body you will see that you are covered with soft, fine hair. When you are cold and you shiver, like the boy in the picture, each hair stands up on end. Little bumps appear all over your skin, too, which are called goosepimples.

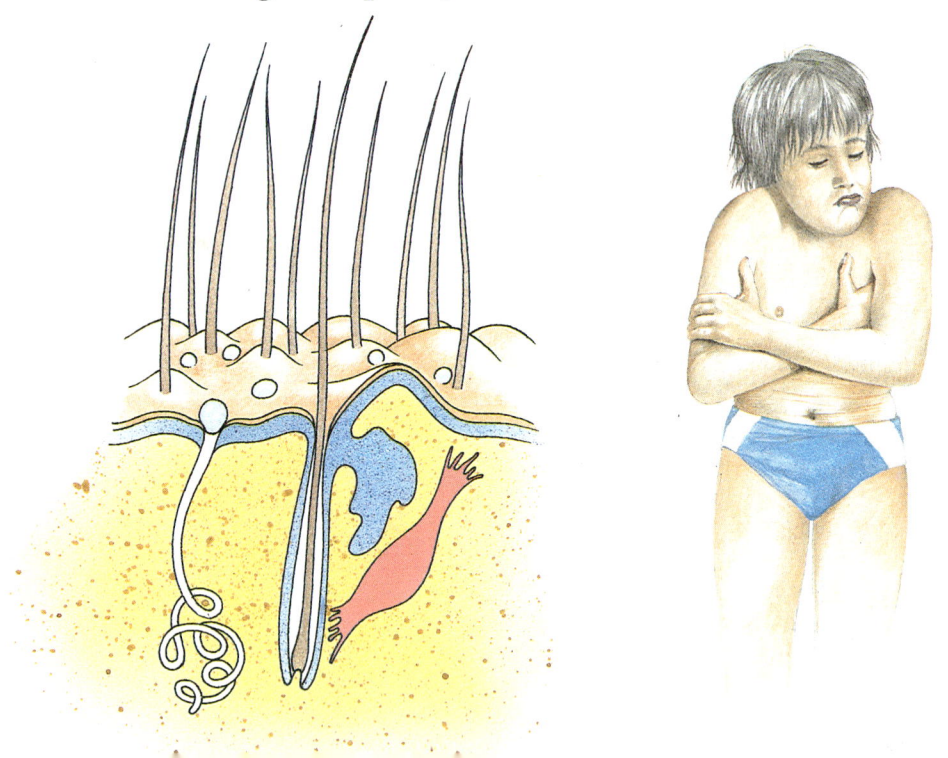

The hair of your eyebrows and eyelashes is thicker than the rest of the hair on your body. Your eyelashes are very important to the protection of your eyes. If something as small as a speck of dust touches them your eyelids automatically close. The boy in the picture has closed his eyes quickly to keep the water out of them.

Your eyebrows protect your eyes too, by catching anything that might trickle down your forehead.

How quickly does hair grow?

Your hair grows all the time, but it grows faster at some times than at others. In the winter your hair grows slowly. On the average the hair on your head grows about 1 centimeter (½ in) in a month. The hair on your body does not grow as fast as this.

Each hair has only a certain length of life. Hairs grow for about two to six years and then they become separated from their roots. When you comb or brush your hair these dead hairs will fall out. You can lose up to 100 hairs every day.

At any time the hairs on your head are all different lengths because they are all at different stages of growth. To keep your hair looking at its best, you should have it cut every four to six weeks to remove all the straggly ends.

What kind of hair do you have?

There are many different kinds of hair. Have you got straight, curly, wavy, blond, brown, red or black hair? Whether your hair is curly or straight depends on the shape of each hair. If you could cut a hair in half and look at it under a **microscope** you could see its shape.

Your hair gets its color from **pigments** in the hair follicles. As you get older, sometimes the color gets weak and gradually the hair turns gray or even white.

Some people have thick hair and some people have fine hair. This depends on the number of hair follicles there are on the scalp. You cannot change the kind of hair you are born with. You can dye it different colors, or make it curly when it's straight, but these changes don't last forever.

Taking care of your hair

Wash your hair regularly with a good shampoo and make sure that you rinse it well so that no soap is left. It is not necessary to **lather** your hair more than once if you use a good shampoo. If you have **dandruff** washing it frequently using a mild shampoo will help to control it. If it does not get any better your doctor should be able to help you.

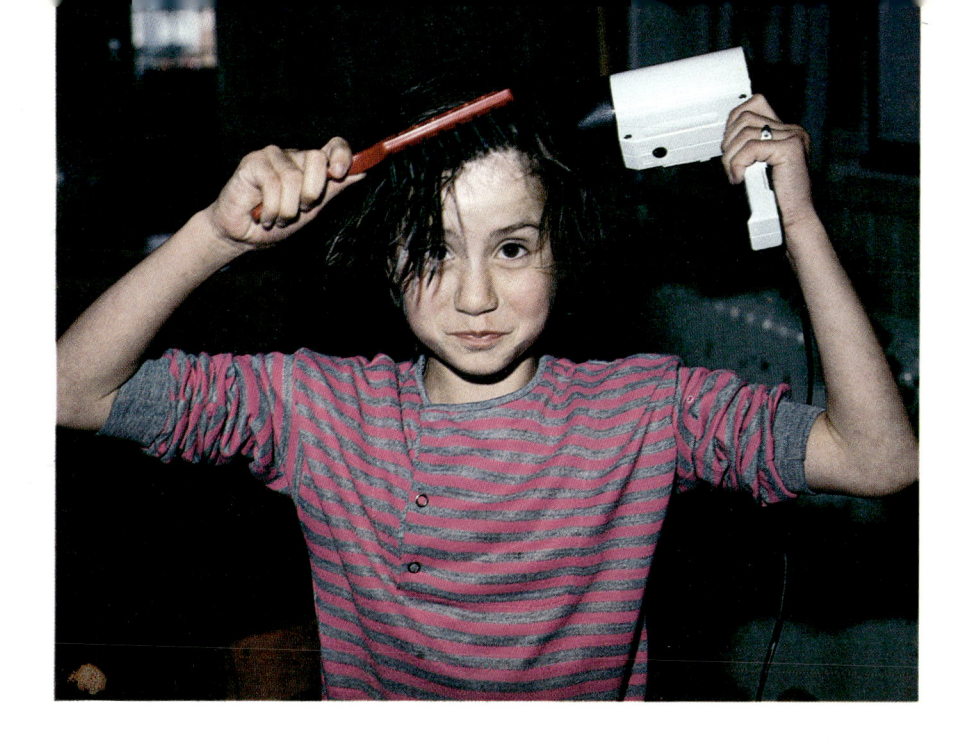

Dry your hair with the drier on a cool setting, so that your hair is not overheated.

Brush or comb your hair twice a day. This removes the dead hairs and any dust that has been caught in it during the day.

To keep your hair looking its best you should have it cut regularly, but don't try to cut it yourself.

It is not a good idea to dye your hair or get a **permanent** very often because you will probably damage your hair.

Glossary

Cells The basic units of living matter; your body is made up of several millions of cells.
Clot A soft lump of drying blood.
Dandruff Flakes of dried skin on your scalp.
Elastic The ability to stretch and spring back again.
Evaporate To change into vapor.
Gland A part of the body that releases different liquids, such as sweat or oil.
Hair follicles The point under the skin from which each hair grows.
Heal To make well again; to cure or mend.
Lather A foam made with soap and water.
Medicated shampoo A shampoo that contains an antiseptic that helps cure dandruff.
Melanin A substance made by your body to protect your skin from the sun.
Microscope A scientific instrument through which very tiny objects can be seen.
Muscle Bundles of fibers that cause movement in your body.
Nerve endings The points in your body where information about your body and its surroundings is collected.
Permanent Short for permanent wave, which is a way of curling your hair.

Pigment The coloring substance in the skin.
Scalp The skin on your head from which your hair grows.
Sensitive Able to feel something easily.
Veins The long tubes which carry blood all over your body.

Index

Baldness 15

Dandruff 22
Dye 23

Eyebrows 17
Eyelashes 17
Eyelids 17

Fingerprints 7

Goosepimples 16

Hair,
   brushing 18, 23
   color 20
   cutting 19, 23
   drying 23
   growth 14, 15, 18, 19
   permanent 23
   washing 22

Melanin 7, 24

Oil gland 15

Scalp 14
Scars 8
Shampoo 22
Skin
   color 7
   healing 9
   sense of touch 4, 11
   stretching 9
Sleep 12
Sweating 9, 10

Touch 4, 11

Veins 6

Washing 12